Giles Swayne

FOUR CHRISTMAS CAROLS
Op. 77

Starlight (1981)
The two Nowells (1999)
Joseph's Carol (2003)
The Coventry Carol (2005)

NOVELLO

FOUR CHRISTMAS CAROLS, Op. 77

Although these carols were written at various dates and are very different from one another, they have two things in common: they are all quite simple, and they all touch in some way on issues of our time.

Starlight (1981) takes a space-age view of the Nativity story, and uses a folksy ballad style to call for global peace. *The two Nowells* (1999) is a revisitation of *The First Nowell*, but adds a bimillennial gloss in the form of *The Second Nowell*. This time around, it is poor children (in the spiritual sense) who are lying awake in over-excitement at the prospect of the electronic delights and computer joys of their presents. Considerably shocked by their greed, the angel reminds them that while one half of the world gobbles its goodies, the other begs for crumbs on the desert floor. Old and new Nowells are then brought harmoniously together for the last verse.

Joseph's Carol (2003) is the Bethlehem story as related by Joseph to his mates in the pub shortly afterwards. I think of him as a Yorkshireman, but he could be from any place that enjoys blunt speaking and dry wit (performers should feel free to adapt the dialect accordingly). *The Coventry Carol* (2005) is a setting of the medieval mystery-play account of King Herod's massacre of the innocents; I have tried to capture the savagery of the infanticide thugs, and the anguish of the children's mothers. Far too many children are still dying every day from starvation, cruelty, and wicked wars. Christmas is a good time to remember these things.

GILES SWAYNE
July, 2005

CONTENTS

	Page
Starlight	1
The two Nowells	3
Joseph's Carol	8
The Coventry Carol	12

Starlight

Words and music
by GILES SWAYNE
Op. 77 No. 1

1. Star of the win-ter night, Where have you been? Why do you burn so bright? What does it mean? Star of the win-ter night, Teach me to share your light And un-der-stand the sight That you have seen.

2. Peo-ple of Pla-net Earth, Hear what I say: God sends you Je-su's birth On Christ-mas Day. Com-fort and joy he brings, Peace, hope and love he sings, Driv-ing the Dev-il's wings Far, far a-way.

3. Stars look-ing back at me, Burn-ing so bright, Shine through the ga-la-xy, Spread-ing your light. Fill ev'-ry part of space with Je-su's love and grace: Bless all the hu-man race On Christ-mas night.

Star - light   is   spread - ing a - cross the sky   To - night   we're

read - ing a mes - sage by   Star - light   and the mes - sage is

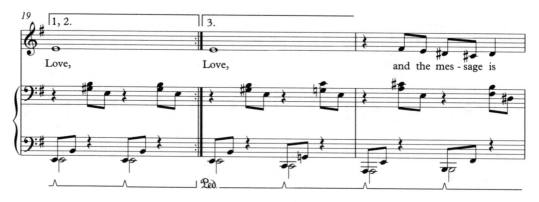

Love,   Love,   and the mes - sage is

Love,   and the mes - sage is   Love.

to Stephen Gilling with many thanks, and in fond memory of Norah Gilling

The two Nowells

Traditional words; new words
by Giles Swayne

Traditional English carol,
arranged and extended
by GILES SWAYNE
Op. 77 No. 2

THE FIRST NOWELL

Quite brisk [♩ = 104]

1. The First Nowell the angel did say Was to certain poor shepherds in fields as they lay; In fields where they lay keeping their sheep, On a cold winter's night that

looked up and saw a star Shining in the east, beyond them far; And to the earth it gave great light, And so it continued both

star drew nigh to the north-west; O'er Bethlehem it took its rest, And there it did both stop and stay Right over the place where

4

was____ so deep:
day____ and night:
Je - sus lay:

No - well,____ No - well,   No - well,____ No-

- well,____   Born is the   King____ of   Is - ra - el.

[1, 2.

2. They____
3. This____

[3.

- el.

THE SECOND NOWELL

mp

1. The____   se - cond   No -
2. They____   lay____   wide   a -
3. "Two____   thou - sand   long
4. While the   poor____   scrimp   and

p

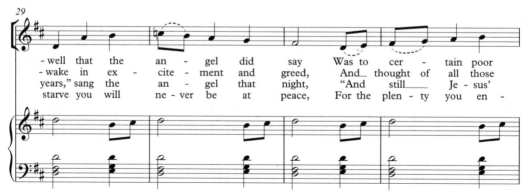

- well that   the   an - gel   did   say   Was to   cer - tain   poor
- wake   in   ex - cite - ment   and   greed,   And__ thought of   all   those
years," sang   the   an - gel   that   night, "And   still____   Je - sus'
starve you   will   ne - ver   be   at   peace, For the plen - ty you en -

chil - dren on Christ - mas day.___ On__
pre - sents they so bad - ly need:___ E - lec-
mes - sage has shed no light:___ One__
- joy___ makes their pain in - crease.___ So__

Christ - mas mid - night they lay try - ing to sleep, But__
tro - nic de - lights and com - pu - ter joys; New__
half of your world hoards rich good - ies ga - lore, While the
o - pen your hearts to all peo - ple on earth: This__

no - thing would work, e - ven count - ing sheep.___
bi - cy - cles, new games and_ new plas - tic toys.___
oth - er begs for crumbs on_ the de - sert floor.___ No -
is the great - est mes - sage_ of Je - sus' birth."___

- well,___ No - well, No - well,___ No - well.___

Born is the King___ of Is - - ra - el.

THE TWO NOWELLS

- el. Then___ let___ us___ all with___ one___ ac -

Then___ let___ us give thanks to the

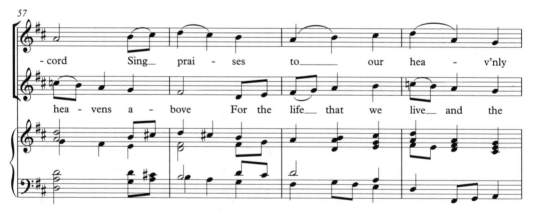

- cord Sing___ prai - ses to_____ our hea - v'nly

hea - vens a - bove For the life___ that we live___ and the

Lord That___ hath_____ made heav'n and___ earth___ of

world we love._____ And___ God___ help man - kind in His

naught, And with His blood mankind hath

wisdom and grace To make our poor planet a

bought. No - well, No - well, No - well, No -

kind - er place. No - well, No - well, No - well, No -

- well, Born is the King of Is - ra - el.

- well, Born is the King of Is - ra - el.

Joseph's Carol

Words and music
by GILES SWAYNE
Op. 77 No. 3

1:When first we came to Beth - le - hem, The snow were fall - ing
Ma - ry woke me up, and said The babe were on its

fast._ We tried the pubs, but none of them Had room, and so at
way._ I roused my - self, and made a bed From bales of straw and

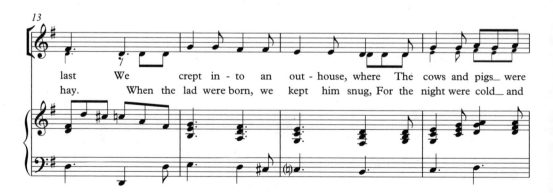

last We crept in - to an out - house, where The cows and pigs_ were
hay. When the lad were born, we kept him snug, For the night were cold_ and

kept. It were warm and dry, so the wife and I lay down a-while, and
raw. So we rolled him up in a ho-ley rug We found up-on the

slept.
floor.   *Glo* - - - - - - - -

- - - - - - - - - - *ri* -

a!   2:Now

3:The sto-ry sounds a wee bit odd, But that's how it be-

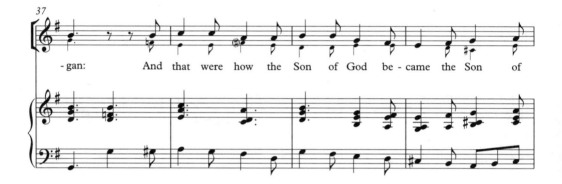

-gan: And that were how the Son of God be-came the Son of

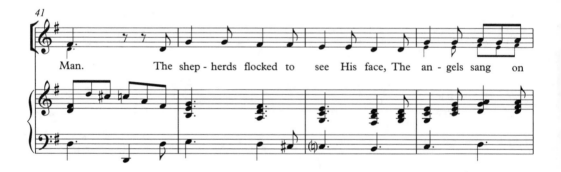

Man. The shep-herds flocked to see His face, The an-gels sang on

high, And He will guard us with His grace Un-til the day we

to Orlando and Delia with all my love, on their engagement

The Coventry Carol

Words:
anon, 16th century

GILES SWAYNE
Op. 77 no. 4

18

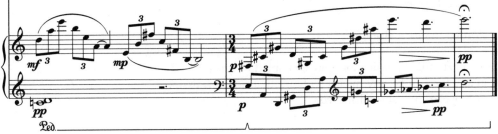

NOV050204
ISBN: 1-84609-183-7

© 2005 Novello & Company Limited
Published in Great Britain by Novello Publishing Limited
(a part of the Music Sales Group)

HEAD OFFICE:
8/9 Frith Street,
London W1D 3JB,
England

Tel +44 (0)20 7434 0066
Fax +44 (0)20 7287 6329

SALES AND HIRE:
Music Sales Distribution Centre,
Newmarket Road,
Bury St. Edmunds,
Suffolk IP33 3YB
England

Tel +44 (0)1284 702600
Fax +44 (0)1284 768301

www.chesternovello.com
email: promotion@musicsales.co.uk